Kidstuff
For
Grownups

*Mary,
May God keep,
"Kidstuff" always in
your heart.*

SECOND PRINTING

*Jean
Holley*

Lamar Holley

Kidstuff
For
Grownups

Lamar Holley

PUBLISHED BY:
BRENTWOOD CHRISTIAN PRESS
4000 BEALLWOOD AVENUE
COLUMBUS, GEORGIA 31904

Dedication

To my family: My loving wife, Jean; our three sons of whom I am extremely proud, Greg, Jim and Bill; our two beautiful daughters-in-law, Dedie and Nelda; and our three adorable grandchildren, Jake, Sam and Lauren. For the joy you bring to me, I dedicate *Kidstuff For Grownups* to you. May we continue to build a legacy of family love and laughter.

Acknowledgements

The stories from which the devotional thoughts in *Kidstuff For Grownups* spring are precious family heirlooms handed down to me over the years. To the friends who shared with me the wit and wisdom of their sons and daughters, their nieces and nephews, their grandchildren or the kids next door, I am indebted. I am blessed and honored that you entrusted your treasure with me.

Much of the kidstuff in these pages grew up with my own family. My wife Jean gave me three wonderful sons and with them was born so much joy and pleasure. Jean and I still laugh ourselves to tears over the innocent insight into things spiritual expressed in the words of our boys. For creating a home filled with love and laughter, for her helping me to let the kid inside me come out to play and for her inspiration to complete this publication, I am so grateful to my Jean.

Joe McKever has been extremely gracious in permitting me to use several of his cartoons to illustrate and enliven my writing. I have enjoyed Joe's art since our days in seminary. He would arrive in the theology classroom early and would have a cartoon on the chalkboard to greet the rest of us. Joe

McKever is a gifted cartoonist, and I am thankful that he has allowed me to share his work with you.

Brenda Sue Davis is Administrative Secretary and my ministry assistant at Lawrenceville First Baptist Church. I am deeply grateful to Brenda Sue for originally typing much of this material as articles for submission to the Gwinnett Daily Post and for preparing this manuscript for publication. Brenda Sue has also provided me with stories from her nephew.

Harriett Claxton for several years has encouraged me to publish this book. She nurtured the dream by helping me to believe that the project was worthy and that I was capable. In recent days Mrs. Claxton has been a valuable friend in proof reading the manuscripts and providing skillful insight for which I am deeply appreciative.

Preface

As you read *Kidstuff For Grownups*, I hope you will be able to see the smiling faces and sparkling eyes of the children whose words I share. May you be stirred with a new appreciation of the amazing innocence and absolute magnificence of childhood. Should you be prompted to take up their cause, to determine that in your home, in your city, over the country and around the world children must be loved, respected and protected, my vision will be advanced.

The headlines of the news media present an almost daily report on family life and they indicate that we are failing. Child abuse and neglect are epidemic in the home and the extent of exploitation of boys and girls over the internet is becoming more apparent. The carnal cancer of our culture crawls through the darkness of child pornography and prostitution.

I do not fanaticize that I possess an adequate platform from which to address in a corrective way the problems of those who steal the smiles from the faces of our children. It is my desire that the devotionals presented in these pages will enlarge your heart toward all children everywhere.

It is my personal passion to strive for a world where the present dangers that destroy the innocence of childhood, steal the sparkle from their eyes and the glow from their faces will be diminished. May God grant to each of us a fuller appreciation for the precious lives of the boys and girls around us and His children all around the world.

Proceeds from the sell of *Kidstuff For Grownups* will be used to support Concern for Kids and other ministries to children.

Table of Contents

Sunday Fishing

During the early years of my ministry, a family with whom I had made several visits decided to join the small church I was serving as pastor.

It was a joy to have the privilege of baptizing the father, mother, son and daughter in the same service. The whole congregation was thrilled our church was growing.

For months, they seldom missed church. Then, it began to happen. They gradually were absent more and more, until they missed more often than they attended.

After an extended period of absence, the father stopped to speak to me at the close of the service. He told me their family had gone to the lake the previous weekend.

On Sunday, they were up early and out fishing. For several hours, they had fished faithfully but caught nothing. The fish were just not biting. Little five-year-old Kathy broke up their boredom by announcing, "I know why we ain't catching no fish; they're in Sunday School where we are supposed to be."

Hearing this story I was reminded of the time when my nephew asked me, "Uncle Lamar, does your church have a uh a uh an aquarium?" He intended to say baptistery, but if

Jesus has called us to be fishers of men, maybe it's not too far off to call our baptismal pool an aquarium.

It was through such experiences that my column, "Out of the Mouths of Babes," was born. I have been excited to have had an opportunity to share my stories. Many have encouraged me to put a collection of those stories in a book. So what if for the most part, they are the parents, grandparents, aunts and uncles of the bright and beautiful kids I have quoted. These are the words of the little folks that have made me laugh and grow to love children as the special gifts from God that they truly are.

When the innocence of childhood speaks with spiritual insight, the words are like precious jewels. Come, let me show you my treasure chest.

What Would Jesus Do?

Knowing of my delight in the unabridged honesty that can flow from the mouths of children, our son Jim called recently to share an interesting story. His girlfriend's young cousins had been playing in a sandbox when their play turned to conflict.

One child came running to his mother reporting that his brother had thrown sand into his eyes. "And what did you do?" she asked. "I threw sand back at him," came his reply. "Well," asked the mother, "What do you think that Jesus would have done?"

The little fellow thought for a moment and then responded, "I think Jesus is too big to play in the sandbox."

What would Jesus do? For several years a lot of young people have been wearing bracelets with the letters, WWJD. The letters symbolize that searching question, "What would Jesus do?" We should be willing to submit every action, every choice to that consideration.

Most of us, whether or not we personally acknowledge faith in Jesus Christ as the Son of God, express admiration for His sacrificial life. He placed others above Himself and served others with a willing spirit.

The life that Jesus lived and the lessons He taught present a powerful example for us to follow. For those who profess personal faith in Christ, His way points out our path of life. He becomes the pattern for all that we are and do.

The man who says, "I have fellowship with Him (Jesus), but does not do what He commands is a liar, and the truth is not in Him" (1 John 1:3-6). This is how we know we are in Him: whoever claims to live in Him must walk as Jesus did.

Many of us are not comfortable with the idea of God getting right down into the sandboxes of our lives. We prefer keeping Him at a distance. So we consider the Creator too big to fit into the crevices and corners of our daily circumstances.

Could it be that we don't want Him watching us throw sand at others or seeing how we are building our lives on shifting sand rather than the solid rock? What would Jesus do? If we are going to measure our lives by His, we must welcome Him into our sandbox as well as our sanctuary.

There Are Songs in There

A grandmother was keeping her young grandson while his parents were out of town. As the grandchild walked through the home with his grandmother, he reached over and touched the keys on the old family piano. Looking up toward his grandmother he said, "There are songs in there, Grams." Then he asked, "Do you know how to get them out?" To the disappointment of the little fellow the grandmother had to admit that she didn't know how to get the songs out of the piano.

Most of us have thrilled in the magnificent performance of a concert pianist, and too many of us have cringed through our children's first recitals. Our pain was not from the discordant sound of wrong notes but from our heart-rending identification with the child's frightful contortions from the piano stool. While we would have wanted every-one in the audience to stand in thunderous approval, that would have to wait until another night. For the time being it was enough that it was finished and we could help our aspir-ing maestro to feel loved and secure.

Between the beginner recital and Carnegie Hall there are many hours of intensive practice. In order to "get the songs out" in an orderly fashion one must spend hours working on the fundamentals of playing the piano. It takes study and practice with such repetition that the process can be painful, but there is no other path to the polished performance.

The writer of Ecclesiastes could have been a good piano coach especially at the point of giving one's best to the practice sessions. He wrote, "Whatever your hand finds to do, do it with your might" (9:10). Those are good words on which to build our lives. There are no shortcuts to a prosperous and purposeful life.

Just recently I learned of a young man who was an outstanding student during his middle school years, but later he lost interest in school and refused to apply himself. Neither school nor church seemed important as he spent his time on fun and pleasure. He is now having to settle for life's second best because of some wrong choices and wasted years. Perhaps there can be a recovery of dreams that are equal to the young man's early potential, but right now he just wants to kick himself.

Precision in performance demands passion in preparation. Why not begin with God's guidebook? Study the Biblical lessons. Put them into diligent practice in your life. God will enable you to "get the songs out." He placed them there, and God is the key to getting them out.

Not Perfect Yet

Before our boys were busily involved with Boy Scouts, Jean and I would occasionally plan camping trips for the family. On one particular trip we had permitted each of our three sons to invite a friend to come along.

Arriving at a lake belonging to a family in our church, we set up our campsite and then started fishing. The fishing was not very successful but the hamburgers grilled over an open fire were sumptuous.

After supper my wife and I went to our tent and the boys and their friends sat outside of their tents and became involved in a discussion that Jean and I have enjoyed through the years.

We heard Jason ask, "What does it mean when you get baptized and become a Christian?" One of the other boys answered, "It means you don't sin anymore." Our Jim, who had observed his older brother since he had made his profession of faith in Christ and been baptized a couple of months earlier, quickly responded, "Unh, unh; that ain't what happened to Greg."

Only a little brother could recognize the cold hard facts and spill it to your best friends. The truth is none of us reach perfection this side of heaven.

The Apostle Paul wrote, I have a desire to do what is good, but I cannot carry it out. Specifically he mentioned how sin was so deceptive as to seize every opportunity to produce in him every kind of covetous desire. Paul said that what he did was not the good that he wanted to do (Romans 7:19). He attributed the inability to live above the grasp of evil to the power of sin that continued to live in him.

In desperation and insight Paul confessed "What a wretched man I am!" and asked "who will rescue me from this body of death?" "Thanks be to God - through Jesus Christ our Lord," he shouted (Romans 7:24-25). That's the answer; that's the solution. We can't but God can.

We can't live above sin. We are not perfect. Yet through the Grace of God and the death of His Son we are covered with a perfect sacrifice of Christ on Calvary.

Golden Excuses

It was such a delightful interruption, and while I had asked for it, I was gloriously surprised. The beautiful little girl spoke out right in the middle of my sermon and her voice carried strongly across the Sanctuary.

I was preaching on the Ten Commandments and my series had led to the third great standard that God presented to His people. The commandment instructed the followers of God that they were to make no idols or images to worship. Jehovah was unwilling to share their affection with any other god.

To illustrate the point I was trying to make I called attention to an event that happened when Aaron had been left in charge of the camp as Moses went up to Mount Siani to receive the commandments from God. The people came to Aaron and asked him to make them an image to worship. At his instruction they brought gold and silver jewelry from their homes. An image in the form of a golden calf was produced and the people bowed down to worship and got up to enter into unrestrained sex games.

Moses returned to the camp and demanded an explanation of what was happening. Aaron reported to Moses that the people had brought their gold and silver and that he threw it into the oven and "lo and behold" it came out in the form of a calf.

I looked out over the congregation and asked, "Now do you really think that is what happened? Did they just throw their jewelry into the oven and out popped the golden image in the form of a calf?"

"No!" the little girl said. Her response from the fourth row rang throughout the building. I hadn't expected an answer but I got one. It was loud and clear and wonderful. I stopped and thanked her before continuing with the sermon.

How many of us tell ourselves and others falsehoods to cover up the irresponsible actions of our lives? Maybe we should listen closely to the excuses that we offer as denials of our unwise choices and disobedient behavior. Could it be that even a child can see through the fog of our dishonest fabrications?

Jewelry doesn't just jump out of the fire fashioned like a golden calf. Neither does most of the junk in our lives just happen.

The man who knows right from wrong and has good judgment and common sense is happier than the man who is immensely rich! For such wisdom is far more valuable than precious jewels (Proverbs 3:13-14 TLB).

With God You Are Able

One of my young doctor friends had to put his car in the shop a couple of years ago to get some much needed repair work done. Unlike most of us, shiny new cars had never seemed all that significant for the young doctor. He was buying his way into an existing practice and had chosen to get as many years as possible out of the old Buick that had driven him through medical school.

While the doctor's car was in for repairs, he was provided a loan car that happened to be several years newer and a few shades brighter than his old Buick. The doctor's young son was so impressed with the loan car that he set in to persuade his dad to buy a new car. For several days the discussion grew with intensity. Finally the exasperated dad said, "No, absolutely not. We are not going to buy a new car right now." With his lower lip "poked out" in a pathetic pout little David responded, "And you call yourself a doctor!"

David had picked up on the belief that those spaces reserved for the doctors looked like the sales lot at a Mercedes Benz dealership. There were some possibilities that went with the vocational territory that his dad had not seemed to grasp.

A lot of folks become so submerged in the problems of life that they never reach up to the possibilities that exist around them. The Bible tells of such an experience. When Moses sent twelve men to Kadesh-Barnea to search out the land that God had promised them, the majority couldn't see the possibilities because they were blinded by the problems they encountered. They saw themselves as grasshoppers in contrast to the inhabitants of the land. The minority group saw a challenge and said, "We are able." The majority saw gigantic problems and cautioned "We are not able to go up against the people; for they are stronger than we" (Numbers 13:30-31). Two men brought back grapes and ten men returned with gripes.

When we look a problem in the face, we should learn to see the potential it presents. Life's challenges do provide us opportunities that demand courage. The boost of our courage, however, is a confidence in God's presence. With God all things are possible.

The Truth

When our son Greg was only six years old, he came into the bathroom where I was shaving and began to tell me about how Jesus had gone down to the Sea of Galilee and said to some of the men, "Follow me and I will make you fishers of men."

Pleased he had been attentive in Sunday School and his teacher had made a strong impression, I asked him, "Son, who told you that story?" He responded quickly, "That ain't no story, Daddy; that's the truth."

Not only had the little fellow learned some Scripture, but he also had learned a high respect for God's Word. It wasn't just a book of fables and fairy tales; it was the truth.

II Peter 1:19-21 reads, "And we have the word of the prophets made more certain and you will do well to pay attention to it, as to a light shining in a dark place, until the day dawns and the morning star rises in your hearts. Above all, you must understand that no prophecy of Scripture came about by the prophet's own interpretation. For prophecy never had its origin in the will of man, but men spoke from God as they were carried along by the Holy Spirit."

We would do well to know we can build our lives on the trustworthiness of God's Word. It's not just a book of stories; the Bible is His story and it is the truth.

As we face the future, this would be a good time to consider looking to the Bible as our road map. Let's allow God who created us to chart our course toward a better and brighter future.

New Direction

In my first pastorate, there was an attractive couple with three beautiful, young daughters. They were part of a large farming family with grandparents, aunts, uncles and cousins, all living in close proximity.

One day, when the father of the three girls came in from the field for lunch, he discovered Sonya, the middle daughter who was four years old, with no clothing above her waist playing with a bunch of neighborhood boys and girls in the front yard.

"Young lady," the concerned father said, "get back in the house and get a shirt on."

Sonya said, "But Daddy, Alan doesn't have on a shirt."

The father sternly replied, "Yes, but Alan is a boy and you are a girl."

Little Sonya innocently retorted, "I haven't decided which one I'm going to be yet."

Have you decided what you are going to be? It is wonderful that we live in a land where we have much freedom to pursue our ambitions and follow our dreams.

I was inspired by the comments of Methodist minister, Dr. Jack Key, at Ed Gannaway's memorial service. Ed was the pilot who died in the crash of a commuter flight near Carrollton, Georgia several years ago.

Dr. Key told of the moment of decision in each man's life when he and Ed listened to the other's dream and encouragingly said, "Go for it." For Ed, that meant a career change to become a pilot. For the retired minister, it meant an adventuresome trip to teach English in China.

The Apostle Paul acknowledged he had not reached all of his goals, but he was quick to speak of his commitment to forget the things of the past and press on toward the future (Philippians 3:13-14).

The Christian faith enables us to experience forgiveness and overcome the failures and frustrations of yesterday.

Faith opens the door to the future. Maybe it is time to make some life-changing decisions.

Did You Say "Adultery"?

Jean had driven our two older sons to their swim team practice. They swam for the Sylvania Sharks and thought they looked fantastic in their green Speedo swim suits. Quickly the boys jumped out of the car and ran to the pool to join the team. Our youngest son, Bill, was left to follow along with his mother.

As they started across the road toward the pool, Bill said, "Come on Mama, let's run." Jean responded, "Slow down, I can't run." Bill answered, "I know why you can't run." "Why can't I run?" my wife asked. Bill's reply startled her and left us with one of our most laughable memories. "Because the Bible says, 'Thou shall not commit adultery'," he spoke in a preaching tone.

Jean's head spun on her shoulders as she inquired, "What does adultery have to do with anything?" Our four year old looked up and asked, "Ain't that when grownup people run around?"

Okay, he had it a bit confused but he was learning. It is vitally important that we share our faith and values with our children.

In the Old Testament book of Deuteronomy, God directed His people to "Fix these words of mine in your hearts and minds... Teach them to your children, talking about them when you sit at home and when you walk along the road, when you lie down and when you get up."

Today's self-help psychology books are filled with helpful hints and suggestions, but we must rediscover the timeless traditions of the Bible. The truth of God's Word provides the strong foundations that our floundering culture and failing family life needs. God's directions for building our lives are not called suggestions but The Ten Commandments.

When God's people, Israel, broke these commandments and began to worship other gods, He charged them with spiritual adultery. God even called upon His prophet, Hosea, to marry a woman who was a harlot. When, after bearing Hosea's children, Gomer chose to return to her adulterous lifestyle, God sent Hosea out to the market place to buy his wife out of whoredom. What a wonderful drama of the loving heart of God.

Right on down through history God has continued to express His redeeming, life changing love. "But God demonstrates his own love for us in this: while we were still sinners, Christ died for us" (Romans 5:8).

Athens, Georgia or Heaven

Bill was an avid Georgia fan. If the Dawgs were playing in Athens, he was there. His family held season tickets and had a host of tailgate friends. University of Georgia football was serious fun.

Dressed out in red and black with the station wagon parked in its usual place, football Saturdays were Fall festivals. Before game time it was party time with an abundant supply of the South's best fried chicken, baked beans, potato salad and banana pudding.

While in Athens for a big game Bill's chest tightened; pain coursed through his shoulder and down his arm. His faced paled, he slumped and he died.

Three days later the family and friends huddled in a cemetery in their small hometown in south Georgia. A red and white casket was slowly lowered into the ground. Uga, our favorite bulldog and I don't know which number, was in attendance. His moist eyes and wrinkled face expressed the loss felt by family and friends.

After the funeral the family returned to their home. A grieving grandmother took a tearful grandson into her arms and asked, "You do know where Grandpa has gone; don't you?" The little fellow looked a bit perplexed and then offered a response that has left the family rolling with laughter ever since. "He's gone to the University of Georgia," was his reply. That wasn't a bad guess for a little guy given all the confusing signals.

Throughout all recorded history and almost universal to every culture there have been evidences of a belief in life after death. There is an eternal quality to the human soul, a divine nature that drives us to soar beyond the boundaries of earthly existence.

The Bible addresses that longing of the soul. "If only for this life we have hope in Christ, we are to be pitied more than all men" (I Corinthians 15:19). Paul had already stated that if Christ had not been raised, our preaching and our faith is useless. But he went on to affirm that Christ has indeed been raised from the dead. Elsewhere he assured us that we can "know that if the earthly tent we live in is destroyed we have a building from God, an eternal house in heaven, not built by human hands." (II Corinthians 5:1)

Even calculated in "Dawg" years, life here has its limits. Yet, through faith life has no limits. We are made for eternity. In fact God has set eternity in the hearts of men. We are forever people.

If It Ain't Broke

The telephone rang and the young mother of three pried herself from her children's grasp and answered it. "Sandra, my water broke and Bob and I are on the way to the hospital." That was all it took to set in motion the plan for Sandra to get to the hospital to share in the birth of her sister's first child. But with Sandra's husband, who is a pastor, being away from the home, a baby sitter had to be called. Several times the message was repeated, "My sister Allison's water broke and she's at the hospital. Could you come over and stay with the kids?" With a sitter secured, Sandra rushed to the hospital.

Later that evening the father returned home to find a baby sitter with the children. She explained, "Sandra's sister's water broke and they've gone to the hospital." The baby sitter was paid and relieved of her responsibilities, and the dad took charge. It was bath time, story time, bedtime and prayer time.

But it was not just a "Now I lay me done to sleep" kind of prayer. It was serious; it was urgent. Five year old Andrew kneeling beside the bed and bowing his head to the floor pleaded, "Dear God, please help Aunt Allison's water to get fixed."

We have all heard the Southern maxim, "If it ain't broke, don't fix it." Broken is not always bad. There are times when broken things are healthy. The water had to break for the baby to be born.

The psalmist wrote, "The sacrifices of God are a broken spirit; a broken and contrite heart, O God, you will not despise" (Psalm 51:17). The way of brokenness is the pathway to spiritual blessing. Arrogance and human pride bloat our self-sufficiency and block the channels of grace. Humility touches the heart of God and God reaches out His healing hand of mercy to cleanse our hearts and renew our spirits.

God responds with amazing grace to our broken spirits and reaches through our brokenness to bless others.

A Child Shall Lead Them

A young mother asked if I would be available to talk with her daughter about joining the church. The precious eight year old was wanting to make a profession of faith in Christ and to be baptized. Indeed I would be available, eager actually. Leading little ones to receive Christ as their Savior is the most delightful responsibility of my ministry. Helping folks to find a personal relationship with the Lord is a great joy.

I do not always know when a person is going to walk to the front of the Sanctuary at the decision time to make a commitment to Christ, and that is as it should be. There must always be room for the Holy Spirit to move totally apart from our plans and preparations.

However, when it is a child who is ready to receive Christ and unite with the church, he or she will have usually spoken first with a parent who in turn has made me aware of the matter. It was just such a situation when I met with Julie. Her mom and dad brought Julie to my study and remained with us as I talked with her about her decision for Christ.

"When have you had these feelings that you should now accept Christ as your Savior?" I asked Julie. "Was it in

Sunday School, at home in talks with your parents, or in worship as I preached?" "No sir," she said, "it was because of all the shootings." Julie was referring to the attacks in the financial center in Atlanta in which nine persons were killed as well as to the school shootings of last spring. "I want to be sure I will go to heaven; I don't want to go to hell," Julie said.

Wow! That was heavy. Feeling the weight of her words, I began to wallow around in a theological discussion about God's love. "For God so loved the world that He gave His one and only Son, that whosoever believes in Him shall not perish but have eternal life" (John 3:16). There, that softened the situation a bit. I breathed easier.

"You know," Julie said, "we are not ready to live until we are ready to die." Hey, she was stealing my lines. Something in me wanted to say, "Slow down girl, I'm the preacher around here."

Thanks Julie, you got it just right. "Go girl!"

37

A Good Time for a New Start

It was Easter Sunday, and I was stammering my way into the children's sermon. The church was full; it always is on Easter. People come to worship on Easter who attend only rarely throughout the year. I choose never to chastise those Easter worshippers.

While I am disturbed about nominal Christianity and the low level of commitment that mark so many who profess faith in Christ today, I can't unload on those folks who come on Easter. It's the best day and the best news the church has to offer. Jesus is alive!

Now, as I was saying, the church was full. So were the faces of the children who came down the aisle to gather around me. Like a puddle of promise, these bright-faced and colorfully clothed kids poured from the pews for their moment with the preacher. Many times, my eyes have grown moist as I have watched them coming toward me robed in innocence and hope.

There they were, handsome and happy. I began, "You boys and girls look so pretty today all dressed up in your new Easter clothes." From the moment I started that sentence, I knew there was something wrong with it. Little Lionel was quick to respond, "I've got some new clothes at home, but my mother wouldn't let me wear them today." I was not sure he did, but I was absolutely certain I wished I could take that one line back and start over again.

It's not a new Easter outfit that's important. When we understand what Easter is about—not eggs and rabbits, but life and hope—Easter attire becomes entirely insignificant. The resurrection of Jesus we celebrate at Easter makes it absolutely possible for us to move beyond all of the stammering, stumbling mistakes of our lives and start all over again. By the grace of God and the power of a risen Savior and Lord, we can be clothed in hope for all eternity.

Go to church somewhere this Sunday. It's the best day of the year, and a great time to start over. We are invited to come dirty and torn with the new all worn off to let the living Lord change us and make us new.

Child Care

A burst of thunder sent a 3-year-old little girl running into her parents' bedroom.

"Mommy, I'm scared," she said. The sleepy mother responded, "Go back to bed, God will be there to take care of you." The little girl began walking slowly off to her room but stopped and came back with a brilliant idea.

"Mommy," she asked, "why don't you go in there with God and I'll sleep with Daddy."

In our world, filled as it is with so many storms, the thunder is deafening and the winds are turbulent. Those who are being tossed around the most are our children and youth.

A social-health index was developed by researchers at Fordham University's Institute for Innovation in Social Policy. The results of a recent study were scary. Four of the six problems in the survey affecting young Americans – child abuse, teenage suicide, drug abuse and high school dropouts had worsened.

Another study reveals about 12 million American children go hungry or are threatened with hunger. Only a few weeks ago a local couple was arrested for attempting to starve their young children. Just recently the Department of Family and Children's Services here in Georgia has publicly admitted that they have failed in certain situations to provide adequate protection for children under their care.

I sat with tears in my eyes and watched a television news documentary on the sexual abuse of young teenage boys and girls. Poverty pushed these kids to prostitution and perverted men were traveling half way around the world to purchase the innocence of these young people.

One of the many positive social implications of the great spiritual awakenings that spread through England and America during the mid-nineteenth century was the correction of the abusive use of child labor. Today, we need a fresh movement of God's spirit to ignite in our souls a responsible caring for the well-being of children.

Let's not go to sleep in the face of the storms that are causing so much devastation and pain in the lives of young Americans.

Nothing is more inspiring than to hear a happy, secure child singing "Jesus Loves Me," and there is no greater evil than the abuse and neglect of children that steal their song and dull their smiles. Wake up America!

Color Me Resourceful

The lady's name was Rose and she was a seasoned veteran. The earlier days of a queasy stomach that was characteristic of most newcomers to the school and hospital for the mentally challenged was forgotten. She was a part of the institution and family to her fellow workers as well as to the boys and girls from five to seventy-five who graced the state-operated facility.

I was there as a Summer Chaplain still trying to overcome some of the shock and adjust to the sights, sounds, and smells that were painfully new. Rose stood before the class of new recruits to orient us to the world of the mentally challenged and to the life of the institution. The stories that Rose told and the compassion with which she spoke expressed a great love for the residents and her work with them.

She told us of a young fellow who in coloring a picture in his class used a black crayon to color everything. The trees, the sun, the dog - they were all black. The child's teacher was concerned by this abnormal behavior, and counselors were brought in to see if they could determine what the little fellow's problem might be. They were alarmed at the social and psychological possibilities of such dark expression.

After some lengthy time with the boy one of the psychologists asked him if he would be willing to tell them why he had colored everything black. He responded, "Yes, sir. Johnny chewed up all the other 'trayons'."

Now I'm not absolutely sure of the authenticity of that experience, but I like the story. It speaks of a kid who is willing to work with what he's got.

Life is not like five card draw. We must learn to play the cards we are dealt.

It serves no purpose to ponder the possibilities of what we could have done if we had been placed in better circumstances. One of the clearest of all God's commandments is the one that deals with covetousness.

To allow ourselves to be shriveled up by an envious spirit is to sin against the God who created us. Who would have the audacity to stand before God and say, "What you have given me is not enough." To loathe ourselves with feelings of inadequacy is nothing short of ingratitude.

Splash what you have on the canvas of life. It just may turn out to be a masterpiece.

Don't "Blow It"

We had driven through rush hour traffic from Atlanta to Macon to arrive just in time for the wedding rehearsal. I was to conduct the wedding and Jean, my partner in marriage, was to be the wedding director. Although I had encouraged Jean to leave a work related conference an hour before its conclusion so that we would not be late, we were some of the first of the wedding party to arrive.

The rehearsal started late and wouldn't you know it, the wedding started late too. Just like we rehearsed it. Well, not exactly.

During the wedding the little flower girl, who was just a bit too young for her role, began to stroll from her assigned location. Trying to stay focused on the young bride and groom standing before me at the altar, I lost sight of the flower girl as she circled around behind us.

Whoosh…whoosh…whoosh… I couldn't believe my ears. The darling little girl was trying to blow out the "unity candle." "Please God don't let her do it," I prayed silently as I solemnly continued the ceremony. Bursting inside with laughter I struggled to keep a straight face.

God said of Adam, "It is not good for man to be alone." God's remedy for man's incompleteness was a companion with whom a fulfilling unity might be achieved. Simply going through the ritual of marriage does not accomplish that kind of unity. "Being united" and "building unity" are not the same thing.

Right in the heart of the Apostle Paul's description of love in the thirteenth chapter of I Corinthians, he says "love is patient, love is kind." These attitudes of love put into action in a marriage or family relationship do lead to unity and provide great joy and pleasure in our homes.

Many of us need to become "transition people", as Stephen Covey puts it, and drop the baggage of anger from our past. We must learn to relate to each other with a kind and gentle spirit. There are enough outside wolves blowing against our doors. Let's make certain that we don't huff and puff until we extinguish the unity of our marriages and family relationships.

Don't Waste Yourself

Kodell Thomas is one of those resilient "steel magnolias" who grew up through the lean years of the Great Depression. The winds of financial adversity that swept across her life left a rugged spirit of frugality. The lady is not stingy, just stubbornly saving. The quip "Waste not, want not," could come from her lips as a chilling call to responsibility.

Kodell reminisced about her efforts to instill in her two daughters the grace of sharing and a commitment to frugality. She knew it would build character. Soft drinks were shared. Candy bars were halved. Toys were ours jointly. They must not be wasteful.

Marsha, the younger of the girls, aggravated by the stringent demands, sullenly asked her mom, "When we get married, are we going to have to share a husband?" Kodell snapped back, "Certainly not. You will both have your own husband." Marsha quickly responded, "Well, that sounds like a waste of men to me."

The story of the prodigal son tells of a young man who asked for his inheritance and promptly went out and squandered, or wasted, his new wealth on wild living. It was only when his energies and options were almost gone that he decided to go home. His rebellious spirit was depleted. His pride was spent. The young man remembered his father and turned toward home.

Oblivious to God's grace, many have thrown off all restraint and are wasting themselves. Life for such persons is a selfish pursuit of pleasure. Wasted is a word that young folks use to speak of their friends who are intoxicated with alcohol or drugs.

It is possible that you may be drunk with ambition or driven by lustful desires. Maybe you are striving to stash away enough to retire comfortably but inside there's that uncomfortable feeling of knowing that you are about spent.

Leap out of your "Great Depression." Don't waste the present opportunity to share in God's life-changing love.

Friend, This Is God

Manny and Joel were the best of friends. The little fellows were only four years old on a particular occasion when Joel's mother and grandmother were taking their turn at the responsibility of cleaning the small tabby Episcopal Church of which they were members in Woodbine, Georgia.

While the ladies were busy with their chores, the boys were engaged in an expedition of the church. Manny and Joel found their way into the beautiful little chapel out of sight of the mother and grandmother. The ladies heard the boys and stepped to the door way to make sure the boys were okay and heard an inspiring conversation.

As the little fellows stood in front of the altar Joel said, "God, this is Manny." Then Joel took Manny's hand and pulling him closer to the altar, continued, "Manny, this is God."

As Jesus was walking beside the Sea of Galilee, He saw two brothers, Simon, who was called Peter, and Andrew. They were casting a net into the lake. They were professional fishermen. Jesus said to them, "Come, follow Me and I will make you fishers of men." At once they left their nets and followed Him.

Peter became a great preacher and pointed many people to the Lord. Andrew, of whom we read far less in the scripture than we do of his brother Peter, is however discovered on several occasions bringing people to introduce them to Jesus.

"God, this is Manny...Manny, this is God" - a simple introduction and a profound connection. Thank God for all the Joels around us who take seriously the commission of our Lord to help the people of this world to find a connection with the God's World Eternal.

Have you introduced anyone to God lately?

On a Clear Day

While in Chicago attending a conference at Moody Bible Institute, I had the wonderful opportunity to hear Johnny Ray Watson, a tremendous Christian singer. He sang many of the great old hymns that have communicated the amazing grace of God down through the ages. Before singing one of the hymns, Johnny Ray told of having asked a group of children what color we will be when we get to heaven. One precious little girl looked up into the large friendly black face of Mr. Watson and said, "I think we will all be clear."

We teach our children to sing, "red and yellow, black and white, all are precious in His sight." While this is indeed true, it may well be true that God never even sees the pigmentation that colors our skin.

Once I heard a young school teacher telling of the tragic plight of one of her elementary school pupils. An insensitive person in the room asked about the race of the child. The compassionate teacher responded boldly, "Does that matter?"

To God it certainly didn't matter what color or race the child was. Hurt is hurt in any color. We all matter to Him. As His creation we are all of infinite worth.

Let's be perfectly clear; God cares for each and every one of us. Like a mother of five children loves each as though that one were the only one, God loves each of us.

That understanding should color or perhaps "uncolor" our respect for and relationship with all people. God is no respecter of persons (Acts 10:34) and neither should we allow prejudice and racial hatred to blind us to the value of others.

Let us be clear. We are all transparent before the Almighty God. Man looks on the outward appearance, but God sees right through into our innermost being. He sees our hearts (I Samuel 16:17).

It may well be that we will all be clear in heaven. At least our hearts and minds will be made clear and clean.

God Reigns

I recently learned of a pretty little girl in my former home of Dublin, Georgia, who has a question about the wisdom of God. Jordan has never liked meat. She will not even eat food that has been seasoned with meat. Her uncanny ability to detect the taste of meat flavor in beans and vegetables at such an early age puzzled her parents. But she knew it was in there and she wouldn't tolerate it. She would not eat it.

Now Jordan has learned that meat comes from animals and is repulsed by the very idea of eating animals. She can't stand the smell of meat cooking and is uncomfortable watching others eat meat dishes. Even as the family was enjoying a fish fry, she thought it to be gross.

Jordan's mom attempted to explain to her that God created all things and that He made everything in the world to work together. God made vegetables and fruit for people to eat. He also made animals to serve people. Some animals were created to help people work, like horses. Others are for companionship, like dogs. But certain animals were put on earth for people to eat in order to be strong and healthy. Jordan was thrown into deep concentration. The mother was proud of her mothering skill and her explanation of the wonderful circle of life. Jordan shocked her with the exclamation, "That was so RUDE of God!"

When Job was reeling under the devastating losses that came upon him, he questioned the integrity and wisdom of God. His friends offered their advice and added to Job's confusion.

Then it was God's turn to speak: "Who is this that darkens my counsel with words without knowledge? Brace yourself like a man and I will question you...Where were you when I laid the earth's foundation? Who marked off its dimensions? Surely you know! On what were its footings set, or who laid its cornerstone—while the morning stars sang together and all the angels shouted for joy? Have you journeyed to the springs of the sea or walked in the recesses of the deep? What is the way to the abode of light? And where does darkness reside? Can you bind the beautiful Pleiades? Can you loose the cords of Orion? Who provides food for the raven when its young cry out to God and wonder about the lack of food? (Job 38) Awesome! Wow!

Job responded to God, "I am unworthy—how can I reply to you? I put my hand over my mouth" (Job 40:4).

Let's not try to push our political correctness off on God. The Lord God omnipotent is not rude, He reigns.

Better Than Nothing

One of my older preacher friends enjoys telling the story of the time he and his wife were out for their afternoon walk and had an enlightening encounter with our youngest son. Bill was only five years old at the time, and he thoroughly enjoyed fishing in the lake near our home.

Retired minister W. B. Hoats and his wife spoke to Bill as they circled the lake where he was fishing. As they approached him on their second lap around the lake, the couple noticed Bill's fishing rod was bent almost double, and he was vigorously attempting to land his catch. Coming closer, Hoats watched Bill pull a hooked tree limb up onto the bank.

The minister said, "That's not much of a fish, son." Bill responded, "Yeah, but it's a lot better than nothing."

The writer of the book of Ecclesiastes wrote, "Better one handful with tranquility than two handfuls with toil and chasing after wind" (4:6). The Apostle Paul encouraged the young man Timothy to understand, "Godliness with contentment is great gain." He continued, "For we brought nothing into this world, and it is certain we can carry nothing out. And having food and raiment, let us be content" (I Timothy 6:6-8).

Many of us keep ourselves dissatisfied and unsettled because our want lists are too long. While God promises to give his children the desires of their hearts, it is with the understanding those desires be kingdom dreams.

We must learn a contentment and confidence in regard to our material needs that comes only through a close, personal faith in the Lord. As Christians, we are challenged to not be anxious over anything, but through prayer with thanksgiving share our needs with God. Of course, He already knows what we need better than we do ourselves, and He has promised to meet those needs according to his glorious riches in Christ.

You can trust God. He will not disappoint you.

Trusting him is not only "a lot better than nothing." It's better than anything you can imagine.

Get Me a New Teacher

Ken Ross, a pastor friend of mine, told me of an enlightening conversation with his daughter as she returned home from her first grade class at school. Ken asked her how her day at school had gone. "Daddy," she said, "It was all right I guess, but you are going to have to get me a new teacher. Mrs. Payne asked me my name. Then she asked us if we could tell her what one plus one was and what two plus two was. Daddy, if she doesn't know any of those things, she can't teach us anything."

As the Apostle Paul wrote to the believers in Ephesus he shared that he "keeps asking that the God of our Lord Jesus Christ, the Glorious Father, may give you the Spirit of wisdom and revelation, so that you may know Him better." Paul prayed that the eyes of their hearts might be enlightened so that they might know the hope to which God had called them. Further, Paul asked God to enable them to grasp how wide and long and high and deep the love of God really is and to know this love that surpasses understanding (Ephesians 1:17-18 and 3:17-19).

A lost and lonely world needs to know the love of our Savior and Lord. God has commissioned us to meet that need. We are to be ambassadors for Christ in this world and by His love we have been commissioned into that service. Are you actively sharing the love of Christ with others? Not just by word, but through acts of Christian kindness are you communicating the reality of the faith, hope, and love that is found in Christ Jesus?

The problem is that many of us don't really know the Lord, not in a personal way. We have not grasped the greatness of His grace. If we call His name, it's often in vain. We add two plus two and get seven. We don't comprehend the basics of the Christian Faith. We have not seen for ourselves the glorious hope that is in Christ Jesus.

Jesus said, "If a blind man leads a blind man, both will fall into a pit" (Matthew 15:14). Pray that the Lord will reveal to you His wonderful love. As He does, will you commit yourself to sharing Him with others?

Bothered Mothers, Blessed Children

A young mother shared with me her effort in attempting to teach their two year old the Bible verse "Honor thy father and mother." The words that came back from his lips brought a stunning surprise as he announced "Bother thy father and mother."

As Mother's Day approaches, it will be impossible to erase from our minds the heartbreak and devastating loss of the mothers of the Columbine High School students in Littleton, Colorado. While I am no less concerned for the parents of the twelve students and the family of the teacher who were killed in the violent attacks by the two young disturbed students, my heart aches with the mothers of those two.

While the media discusses whether or not these families can be held liable for the actions of their sons, these parents must be wrestling in self-condemning anguish. They must be asking over and over again "why?" "What could I have done differently?" It would be difficult to imagine these families not being torn with blame and shame. Yet there is so much shared responsibility for the chaotic violence in our society that it would be unconscionable to heap heavier burdens on these parents.

That said, we must acknowledge the role of parents in the development of their children. There is no greater joy than the birth of a child in our homes and there is no greater responsibility. God's instruction to His people was that they "Fix these words of mine in your hearts and minds...Teach them to your children, talking about them when you sit at home and when you walk along the road, when you lie down and when you get up" (Deuteronomy 11:19-20).

With the openness of our society and the corruption of so much of our culture, there are many damaging influences on the lives of our youth. When these influences are allowed to outweigh the Christian teaching of Godly parents and church involvement, it brings "bother" and heartbreak to mothers and fathers.

I challenge you to become more involved in the lives of your children. Bother to spend time together as a family. Bother to get out of bed and get to church on the Lord's Day. Bother to pray for your children. Bother yourself in order to bless them.

If you have been blessed by a mother's love and care, take time to tell her how much she is appreciated and loved. For all the bother of the past, bless her today.

Bumps Are There
For Climbing

A little boy was leading his sister up a mountain path, and the way was rough and rugged. "Why, this isn't a path at all," the little girl complained. "It's all rocky and bumpy." Her brother replied, "Sure it is. The bumps are just what you climb on."

What a remarkable insight and tremendous spiritual truth. The bumps are, indeed, what we can use for climbing. When our pathway is piled full of rocks, we need to dig in and keep on climbing. If you are beginning to feel like your life is really on the rocks, then it's time to discover the bumps are for climbing.

This truth is expressed too clearly in the Scripture when the Apostle Paul writes, "...we also rejoice in our sufferings, because we know that suffering produces perseverance; and perseverance, character; and character, hope" (Romans 5:4).

Several years ago, I had the opportunity to be back in Anniston, Alabama, and watch (not run in, just watch) a 10-kilometer road race along the streets of my old hometown. While I was interested in watching our son run in the race, my attention became riveted on four racers at the starting line preparing to take off in their wheelchairs. Mutilated by injuries from the Vietnam War and other rough and rugged encounters, now they were preparing to become victors in arm-muscled and iron-mind propelled chariots of a lesser war. Their hearts were big, and their hopes were big.

They were winners before the starting gun ever sounded. The stones that had been thrown in their paths on the other side of the world had not stopped these gladiators.

What do you do when the way gets rough and bumpy? Remember, the bumps are what you climb on. When you think life is on the rocks, look to the Solid Rock and keep on climbing.

An Easter Awakening

Easter provides many opportunities for family and friends to gather for good food and great times. It's an occasion for play as parents hide and children hunt brightly colored Easter eggs. But Easter is not just a child's happy holiday. It is the day that trumpets the rebirth of spring and the hope of new life.

A celebration of the Christian faith in the resurrection of Jesus following His sacrificial death, Easter holds paramount significance for the believer. Those who were the closest friends and relatives of Jesus watched Him die. The cruel crucifixion on Calvary had killed their hope. They hurt, they hid, but they didn't even begin to hope.

His friends hurriedly, halfway performed the duties for the burial and began to ponder how they might rebuild their lives. Their king was dead and the kingdom had come to a sudden end.

Sue Monk Kidd in her book, *When the Heart Wakes*, tells a wonderful story of an Easter tradition in her family. Continuing a practice that she had first learned from her parents, Mrs. Kidd was teaching her daughter how to carefully make a small hole in an egg and blow the contents of the egg from the shell before the egg would be dyed and decorated.

Holding the empty shell in her hand the daughter asked, "Could there have been a baby chicken in there?" Mrs. Kidd explained that if the egg had been left with the mother chicken longer, it could have developed a baby chicken inside the shell. Her daughter responded, "I wish we had left it longer; I think I would like a baby chicken."

Without the Easter truth Christianity would be an empty shell. For the Christian, everything we believe and our whole future depends upon the reality of the resurrection.

The Lord's disciples were not quick to believe that Jesus had risen from the tomb.

It seemed all too strange, too unbelievable. A day filled with unexpected appearances in the garden, the upper room, and on the road to Emmaus assured them that Jesus was alive.

Three days they had waited in their pain, not knowing what to expect. Then came the resurrection and with it the renewal of their lives.

Today the risen Lord is still alive. He would want to come into your emptiness and fill your life with hope and purpose. May your heart awake to that reality just now? Invite Him in.

Have a Lot of Fun

"Have a lot of fun Reverend Holley; have a lot of fun!"

I will always remember those words. The little guy who shouted the encouragement to me was Drew, my five-year-old version of "Dennis the Menace" who lived across the street. I was driving out of my driveway in Dublin for the last time when I noticed Drew in his front yard.

Pulling to the curb, I said, "Drew, you know we are moving to Lawrenceville to pastor a new church, but I'll see you again sometime." It was then that Drew yelled back, "Have a lot of fun Rev. Holley."

I probably needed Drew's challenge as much or perhaps more than all of the other well wishes and promises of prayer. It is easy for me, like most folks today, to become so involved in work that it loses some of its joy.

There is a difference between church work and the work of the church. To God's redemptive work through the church I must learn to give my life without allowing the busy work of the church to rob me of adequate family time and recreational time to nurture my soul and renew my spirit.

Have your daily duties become such drudgery that life has lost all of its excitement? Are you having any fun?

While I have not found a full blown theology of fun in the Bible, I believe God planned for life to be pleasurable, and he didn't establish prohibition against having fun.

There is a little child in every one of us who wants to come out and play. Allowing the kid to come out, giving him or her permission to have fun, is achieved through the freedom Jesus, the Son of God, produces within us. Sin and shame tie us in knots and rob us of pleasure. God's loving forgiveness frees us from that bondage. Have faith, my friend, and have a lot of fun.

Investing For Eternity

An aunt who was keeping her young nephew purchased a children's video to help fill the visit with enjoyable experiences for little Andrew. When his aunt pulled the video from her shopping bag, Andrew asked, "When does it have to be back?" The aunt explained that it did not have to be returned. It had not been rented, but bought; it belonged to them and they could keep it forever. "Forever?" the little fellow exclaimed with amazement dancing in his eyes.

Andrew was strangely quiet for about thirty seconds and then he asked in gleeful anticipation, "Aunt Allison, does Jesus have a television?" He may have been only three years old, but already he had begun to think about taking it with him someday.

Jesus said, "Do not store up for yourselves treasures on earth, where moth and rust destroy and where thieves break in and steal. But store up for yourselves treasures in heaven, where moth and rust do not destroy, and where thieves do not break in and steal.

For where your treasure is, there your heart is also" (Matthew 6:19-21).

Recently, I conducted an out of town funeral service. As we left the funeral home, I was invited to ride with the funeral director to the cemetery. As I opened the door to get in, I noticed several coins on the floor mat of the hearse. Teasingly, I said to the funeral director, "I've been trying to teach people for years that they can't take it with them when they die, but now I see you are trying to prove me wrong."

Several years ago I had the privilege of assisting a terminally ill patient at the VA Hospital to make the arrangements to leave all his financial assets, which amounted to just over two thousand dollars, to the Georgia Baptist Children's Home. This gentleman, who had never known his parents and had been shifted from one foster home to another as a child, was choosing that method of making a difference in some child's life. Later as a small group of church friends went to Andersonville Cemetery for Henry's memorial service, we prayed and sang as we watched his remains lowered into the Georgia clay. Having seen Henry give his small holding to a big cause, I stood there thinking that he had stored up some treasures in heaven. Now I'm not suggesting that he took it with him. Actually, I believe he had sent it on ahead.

How about you? Are you sending your treasure on ahead?

Gardening for God

It was one of those absolutely gorgeous spring days when the sun was shining with such brilliance I just had to get out of the office and into the soil. While it wasn't time to be planting vegetables, it was certainly a wonderful occasion to prepare my garden spot for the seeds and sets that would come later.

My little friend Drew from across the street came over to observe what was going on and asked, "Rev. Holley, what are you doing?" I told him I was working in my garden. Without any hesitation, Drew responded, "If you do a good job, I think my daddy will let you make us a garden." You can imagine how thrilled I was at that prospect.

I was reminded of the story Jesus told of a master who entrusted his servants with various degrees of responsibility. Upon his return, the master took away what had been entrusted to the servant who had not been diligent with his responsibility.

To each of those who had been industrious and responsible, the master said, "Well done, good and faithful servant! You have been faithful over a few things; I will put you in charge over many things. Come and share your master's happiness" (Matthew 25.21).

The Bible teaches us that we are laborers together with God. Thomas Carlyle wrote, "Blessed is he who has found his work; let him ask no other blessedness."

Rather than work being a curse, it is indeed a great blessing. While there is a day of eternal rest that awaits us, in this present life, the reward of a job well done is another task to challenge us.

We are instructed to "always give yourselves fully to the work of God, because you know that your labor in the Lord is not in vain" (I Corinthians 15:58). Be faithful as you garden your way through life. My Father will let you work in His garden.

Let God Be Center Stage

Several years ago our son, Jim, had a part in a skit the youth at our church were doing for a Sunday evening service. Although Jim had rehearsed with the drama group, he was becoming frantic because he had not completed a school project that was due on Monday morning.

We overheard Jim trying to talk his older brother into going to the afternoon rehearsal and taking his place in the performance so Jim could work on his school assignment. Of course, the older brother was resisting. He was certain there was no way he could memorize the lines in the short time left.

Jim responded to his resistance by saying, "You don't have to memorize anything. You will be God and you are supposed to stay behind the curtain." He could just read his lines from the manuscript and no one would know any difference.

We understand the point Jim was making. It was the phrase about God staying in the background behind the curtain that caught us by surprise.

Many of us keep God in the background of our lives. We want Him behind the curtain or off stage. We say we believe in a supreme being out there somewhere. We make Him sound far away. Some of us are more comfortable with the distance.

One of the marvelous messages of Christmas is that God chose to come close to us. God wants to participate in our lives. The truth that we celebrate at Christmas is the nearness of God. God came to us in Christ at Christmas.

It is as we allow Jesus Christ to come into our personal lives as a participant that He invades the darkness of our despair and depression and doubt. A personal relationship with Christ brings the light of God's hope to us.

In Christ, God took center stage in human history to say, "I love you." Will you raise the curtain to your life and step into "His-story?" Don't keep Him backstage any longer.

Are You Too Comfortable?

Sarah Grace was only three when her grandmother discovered that she had taken baby Jesus from the nativity scene and carried Him into her bedroom. The beautiful and cogent child was carefully tucking Jesus under the covers.

Wanting to do some teaching the grandmother said, "That's not the way the Bible story goes. When Jesus was born they placed Him in a manger where the cattle ate."

Sarah Grace responded, "I know, but this is a lot more comfortable and He will be safer here." The precious child with such a compassionate spirit wanted the baby Jesus to enjoy the soft comfort and security of her bed and the warmth of her room.

A religious teacher came to Jesus and said, "I will follow You wherever you go." "Foxes have holes and the birds of the air have their nests, but the Son of Man has no place to lay His head," Jesus replied (Matthew 8:19-20).

Comfort was not foremost in the mind of Jesus when through the miracle of incarnation, He left the riches of heaven to take on human form and live among men on earth. Yes, He was born in a cattle stall amid the stench of animal waste, and life did not get a whole lot better.

From casual suspicion of those who thought they knew Him, to the callous rejection of those who refused to know, to the cruel crucifixion by those who didn't have a clue, His life was one of sacrificial suffering.

The apostle Paul said, "I want to know Christ and the power of His resurrection, and the fellowship of sharing in His sufferings."(Philippians 3:10) While most of us are eager to experience the power or strength of our Lord, we do not readily volunteer for pain or poverty.

A life of Christian faithfulness often calls us out of our comfort zones. Are you too comfortable to face the challenge to which Jesus Christ is calling you? Then pull back the covers under which you are hiding, jump out of bed and join Jesus.

My Name Is Will

During Vacation Bible School time boys and girls are running around most of our churches like busy armies of ants. Vacation Bible School is as much a part of summer as the Fourth of July and just about as exciting. Pastors love VBS and the teachers who work with the children endure it. They willingly and sacrificially give their best to the week's work. Many of them neglect household chores, shortchange family responsibility and some even give up vacation time to share the love of Christ with bright eyed boys and girls.

It was on the third day of VBS that I was invited to the five year old class to present their Bible story. The lesson was about Jesus sharing the Passover Meal with his followers and using that occasion to begin what we call The Lord's Supper or Communion to commemorate His death on the cross. I was telling the children of how Jesus prayed as He faced His impending death on Calvary. To His Heavenly Father He prayed, " Not my will but Thy will be done."

A handsome blond headed boy interrupted me. "That's my name," he said. I gazed questioningly toward the young fellow and he said it again. "That's my name; my name is Will." His face glowed with excitement at his connection with the Bible story, and my heart flamed with the thrill of the delight that I could see in his eyes.

It should be each of our desire to understand and to do the will of God for our lives. Philippians 2:13 says that "…it is God who works in you to will and act according to His good purpose." God has a will for your life and by His Spirit He is seeking to make you willing to fulfill His purpose.

Frances Havergal wrote these works in a great old hymn that expresses so well the spirit of Godly willingness. "Take my will, and make it Thine, It shall be no longer mine; Take my heart, it is Thine own, It shall be Thy royal throne."

In the Lord's model prayer He taught His disciples to pray, "Thy will be done." That is a prayer that you not only can pray but also one that you can help answer. Are you willing to do the will of God? I hope your name is Will.

Needed:
Miracles in the Home

One of the senior adults from our church returned from the Georgia Baptist Family Bible Conference with a story that the president of the Georgia Baptist Convention had shared in his sermon.

A Sunday School teacher in his congregation had lined her boys and girls up for a trip to the water fountain. It was the pastor's five year old son who announced loudly, "I'd rather have beer than water."

I suppose a truly precocious child or even a fast thinking pastor would have met the raised eyebrows with something like, "Just trying to follow the example of another great Man who turned water into wine."

We can imagine what the teacher was thinking: "Children only repeat what they hear their parents saying." However, we know that is not actually true. Our children are being impacted for better and for worse not only in our homes but also over the community. The educational system is not the always positive influence it once was and much of the television programming is detrimental to our children.

Perhaps the tragic stories of child abuse, neglect and even murder have shocked us to a new awareness. With a new resolve we must seek to develop healthy homes and loving families. In our dangerous world we must provide safety and security for our children.

Let's work some miracles in the home by turning from anger to kindness, and from selfishness to sacrifice. Love the children; make a miracle happen in your home.

Not Like Me

Brenda Sue Davis, who serves as my administrative associate for pastoral ministry, has served the Lord through her ministry in First Baptist Church for over forty years. Her office is the first stop for many boys and girls as they arrive at the church during the week. Somehow they all learn that Brenda Sue keeps a well stocked candy jar.

Not long ago Brenda Sue brought her four year old great nephew, Chase, by the church office. Walking through the reception area Chase noticed a larger number of boxes that covered the floor. They were shoe boxes filled with gifts to be distributed to boys and girls around the world through Franklin Graham's Samaritan's Purse Ministry.

"What are the boxes for?" Chase asked. Brenda Sue explained that they were for children around the world who would not get any gifts at Christmas unless we send them.

Chase said, "Not like me!" His aunt responded, "No, not like you. You will have plenty."

Most of us are like little Chase; we are blessed, we have plenty. Yet, we may not have reached the level of maturity that provides contentment with our present possessions.

The Bible teaches us that God will supply all of our needs according to His glorious riches in Christ Jesus. Many of us have a difficult time distinguishing between our needs and our wants.

It has been said that the luxuries of one generation become the necessities of the next. But in our day of instant gratification our wants leap ahead of that generational clock. Fads fan our desire into a whirlwind of consumer spending. Some of us buy things that we don't really need with money that we don't really have.

God's Word in such contrast to our extravagant spending says that "godliness with contentment is great gain." The apostle Paul wrote, "Some people, eager for money, have wandered from the faith and pierced themselves with many griefs" (I Timothy 6:10b).

May we know the contentment of understanding how fortunate we are and to be so grateful to God that when we see that face of poverty we, like Chase, can say, "Not like me."

Age: A Crown of Splendor

Our five-year-old son had developed a strong friendship with an elderly lady who was our next door neighbor as well as a member of the church I served as pastor. Once, when we had returned from a vacation, Bill jumped out of our car and ran over to Mrs. Newton's home. He climbed up into her lap and leaned over to kiss her. Teasingly, she asked, "Bill, you don't want to kiss an old ugly lady like me, do you?" Bill said, "Mrs. Newton, you're not old and ugly, but some Oil of Olay might help you a whole lot."

In the Bible, there is a proverb that reads, "Gray hair is a crown of splendor; it is attained by a righteous life" (Proverbs 16:31). The writer of Psalm 92 proclaimed, "They will still bear fruit in old age, they will stay fresh and green..."

I am always amazed and blessed by those who remain so alert and alive into later years of age. Recently, I visited Mrs. Emolyn Bowlby a 104-year-old lady who is one of the most vibrant Atlanta Braves fans in the entire country. Until recent years she would sit alone, in front of her television, where she would explode with excitement when her team made a great play. When Bobby Cox was in the face of the umpire, he had this dear lady backing him up, and there were times when they could likely hear her all the way down to Turner Field.

Mrs. Bowlby was asked at her last birthday party to what she attributed her longevity. Her answer was: "I always lived right and paid the preacher."

As Charles Swindoll said, "God's patriarchs have always been among his choice possessions." Of course, growing old has its headaches and heartaches, but don't think of age as a mistake or oversight. It is God who has decided to entrust you with long life.

If you are too young to appreciate these words but took the time to read them anyway, why not go out and find you an elderly person? Give him or her a hug and a kiss, or a bottle of Olay, okay?

Out of Control

A young attorney friend told me his associate recently came to the office with a great story. Walking into the living room ahead of his mom and dad, their four-year-old son had discovered the family dog chewing on the remote control for the television. It could be said this is evidence television is going to the dogs.

The little guy looked at the dog and exclaimed, "No, no puppy, that's Daddy's." Wouldn't you like to have that film to submit to America's Favorite Home Videos?

I read just the other day that in most homes it is indeed Dad who monopolizes the remote control to the television. Dad is the super channel surfer of the household. Did you know that you can now purchase wrist watches with a TV remote control feature? It could get complicated if everyone in the family had such a timepiece.

It is easy to sink into the sofa and begin to surf the channels. In so doing, we can become lost in the fantasy world of sitcom fictions, sensuous fitness classes, fantastic football, or the absurdities of reality television. There's always something to lock us onto the tube, but if we are not careful, we lose precious family time.

Proverbs 29:11 says that a wise man keeps himself under control. That, of course, must include wise choices in the use of our time. It is remotely possible the reason things seem so out of control today is that we are not applying God's wisdom to our family responsibilities.

It appears to me that the more remote we are as individuals from an intimate relationship with God the more out of control are our lives. When we fear that we are losing control of our own lives, we attempt, even if unconsciously, to control others. That's one sure way to build unhealthy families.

May I share with you a prescription for a healing medication? Here it is: "Let the peace of Christ rule in your hearts..." (Colossians 3:15).

Promise Keeping

The beautiful young bride in planning for her wedding had asked her little nephew to participate in the special occasion. On the night of the rehearsal he came strolling down the aisle waving one arm wildly over his head. As he walked he was making a growling sound. When he reached the rest of the wedding party at the front of the church, they asked him what all the pawing and growling was about. With no hesitation he responded, "I am the 'ring bear'."

David Sisber told of overhearing a conversation between a jeweler and a lady who appeared to be in her middle sixties. "I can't get my ring off" she said. "I'd like you to cut it off, please."

With a ring saw and a pair of pliers the work was quickly done. "We can resize it for you" the jeweler said. "Let me measure your finger."

The woman examined the untanned and indented circle left by the now severed and twisted ring. "In forty-six years that's the first time it has ever been off my finger. I feel sort of naked without it," she said.

The jeweler repeated his offer to resize the now misshapen ring. He assured her that the ring would look as good as the day she first put it on.

"No," the lady finally answered. "We were married forty-six years."

The jeweler said, "I'm sorry," attempting to express his sympathy for what he assumed to be the death of the woman's husband.

She shook her head and continued, "He's got himself a new woman. I don't ever want to wear this ring again." And with that she picked up what was supposed to have been a symbol of eternal love, dropped it in her purse and walked out of the store.

The ring is a symbol of sincerity in relationships. At the altar of marriage it is the pledge of fidelity that should provide the security on which to build a healthy home.

The Bible is clear in saying, "When a man makes a vow to the Lord or takes an oath to obligate himself by a pledge, he must not break his word but must do everything he said" (Numbers 30:2).

Those who keep their vows as a sacred trust are an endangered species. Our world needs fewer "ring bears" and more promise keepers.

Push Power

Our youngest son was not quite four years old the Christmas that his older brothers asked for a go-cart for Christmas. One of the brightly wrapped boxes under the tree that year contained a note that directed our boys to go to the garage where they would find one of their presents.

Tripping over each other the older boys raced down the stairs, through the basement and into the garage. Bill trailed them coming in a distant third. They were thrilled to discover the shiny red go-cart.

As his brothers danced around their new machine imagining the delight it would bring, little Bill sat down in the seat of the shiney new machine. Taking the steering wheel in hand, he turned toward his brothers and said, "Push me."

Being used to only non-motorized push toys, Bill hadn't even dreamed of the power that the go-cart possessed. The boys still remember that morning and laugh as they recall the dawning of dynamic understanding.

Our Lord is a great God and He is mighty in power. As Jesus the Son of God sent His followers out to share their faith He promised His presence and implied an accompanying power. When He would no longer be physically present, the Holy Spirit would empower them for service.

To be sure God does not indiscriminately release His power to us for selfish pursuits. Rather, as we walk in His will and seek to fulfill His purpose, God by His Holy Spirit energizes us for faithful service and fruitful living.

"Not by might nor by power, but by my Spirit," says the Lord Almighty (Zechariah 4:6). Are you pushing and shoving and getting nowhere? Why not turn your heart toward the Lord and allow Him to empower you?

Thanksgiving

A little boy asked his father, "Daddy, if the Pilgrims were really all that religious, why did the men have to carry guns on their shoulders and march their wives and children to church?"

Yes, you've seen that picture too, haven't you? I suppose through the eyes of a child it might look as though it took a great deal of duress to get the family to a house of worship on Thanksgiving Day.

Charles Dickens once said that we are somewhat mixed up here in America. He told an audience that instead of having one Thanksgiving Day each year, we should have 364.

"Use that one day just for complaining and griping," he said. "Use the other 364 days to thank God each day for the many blessings He has showered upon you."

A restless child in an airport was given some candy by a waiting passenger. The child's mother tried to get her son to say "Thank you." The passenger who had been so generous said, "He doesn't have to say 'Thanks'." The mother responded, "But if he learns to, he will be a better person."

God's Word challenges us, "O give thanks unto the Lord for He is good: because His mercy endureth forever"

(Psalm 118:1). We, too, would be better persons if we would glory in the goodness of God and live with a sense of His merciful presence.

Someone suggested that if Thanksgiving Day were not already an established holiday, it would be difficult to initiate such an observance today. There is much evidence that the concept of gratitude is eroding.

Most of us are wonderfully blessed, but too many of us have lost a sense of wonder and are out of touch with the One who is the source of our blessings.

Rather than allowing anxiety to wreck our lives, we need to learn to trust God and to be grateful to Him. We should learn to become less obsessed with our own concerns and more caring of others. Perhaps some act of kindness to others who are less fortunate can best express our sincere thankfulness to God.

Safe and Secure

Some good friends of mine from Dublin, Georgia, recently took their grandsons, Clay and Chandler, out to eat at the Golden Corral. Noticing some folks that he knew sitting across the restaurant, Julian took the boys over to show them off as any proud grandfather would do.

After a short visit at the friend's table, Clay let go of his grandfather's hand and darted over to a door that was armed with a security alarm. He bumped the door setting off an alarming sound that was terrible. The grandfather was quite embarrassed and a little impatient.

The boys were quickly returned to their parents and told that the manager of Golden Corral would probably never let them eat there again.

A few weeks later Clay was with his grandfather again and was asked where he would like to eat. He said, "The Golden Corral, if they will let us." When they entered the restaurant, Julian sent little Clay to ask the manager if they could eat and permission was granted.

As they sat at the table, Clay could be heard singing a tune. The grandfather's close attention detected Clay to be singing the words,..."Leaning on Jesus, Leaning on Jesus, safe and secure from all alarms."

Julian is not absolutely certain that Clay had made the connection between the emergency alarm on the restaurant door and the song he was singing. I can tell you that Clay is a bright little fellow with a strong repertoire of songs. He has been singing amazingly well since he was a tiny tot.

What is truly wonderful is that at such an early age this little guy knows about trusting God, about leaning on Jesus. Clay feels safe and secure.

The Psalmist wrote: "The Lord will keep you from all harm. He will watch over your life; the Lord will watch over your coming and going both now and forevermore." (Psalm 121:6-8)

You can find security in the arms of God's love. Trust Him.

God Likes Preaching

A dear friend of mine, Claude Vines, Jr., grew up in a pastorium. That's where Baptist preachers and their families lived before the churches sold those homes and spread us out over the neighborhoods like real people.

Had Claude's father been a Methodist preacher, he would have been reared in a parsonage, or a manse had he been Presbyterian. Yet, by any other name, the preacher's house is still a fish bowl. Claude, like my own three sons, did enough swimming around to make the dishonorable mention list of the local PKI (Preacher's Kids Inquisition).

Claude was just a little fellow when his father was preaching "up a storm" in a country church in middle Georgia. A lady with a screaming child got up and left the sanctuary (now called the worship center). Claude followed the lady from the services and into the foyer and pleaded, "Lady, please don't spank him. Sometimes, I don't like to listen to him very much myself." You can probably imagine a preacher dad saying, "Thanks, son, I needed that."

There are those who don't like preaching. They think of it as foolishness. Listen to what God's Word says about it.

"For since in the wisdom of God the world through its wisdom did not know him, God was pleased through the foolishness of what was preached to save those who believe" (I Corinthians 1:21). The apostle Paul, understanding that those who called on the name of the Lord would be saved, asked "How, then, can they call on the one they have not believed in? And how can they believe in the one of whom they has not heard? And how can they hear without someone preaching to them?" (Romans 10:13-14).

God likes preaching and made it central to his plan of drawing the world to himself. What the world calls foolishness, God chose as the means of magnifying Christ and proclaiming the good news of his life-changing love.

Let me encourage you to attend church somewhere this week. If it's real gospel preaching, you will come away glorying in the magnificence of the Lord.

Something less may leave you marveling over the minister or worrying about the roast in the oven.

97

Sorry Don't Fix Nothing

Several years ago my wife and our sons traveled with her mother to visit relatives in the Washington, DC area. While in the home of Jean's cousin, they watched as a major conflict broke out between two darling little girls.. The five year old was distraught that her three year old sister had without asking taken her coloring book and with a crayon had scribbled on every page. As far as the older child was concerned, her coloring book was ruined.

In a furious state of rage she pled her case before her mother. The mother turned to the three year old and told her that it was wrong to take her sister's coloring book without asking. "Now, tell your sister you're sorry," the mother demanded. With a pitiful desperation in her voice the violated older sister responded, "Sorry don't fix nothing."

There are times when expressions of sorrow express empathetic concern. The spoken word itself can embrace the broken and bruised victim with the warmth of understanding and offer encouragement and hope.

Just saying "I'm sorry" doesn't seem to be sufficient in the face of hurt and loss. The words don't quite balance the pain inflicted by irresponsible and reckless behavior.

Recently I heard a father tell of hugging his teenage daughter as she shriveled under the heavy pain of rejection. His words to her were, "Honey, Daddy can't fix it, but God can." The resilient young lady responded, "Yes, you are right, I know God can and He will."

The Bible says that Godly sorrow brings repentance that leads to salvation and leaves no regret, but worldly sorrow brings death (2 Corinthians 7:10). Man's greatest problem is that of sin and separation from God. God's solution to that sin problem is salvation or a life transformation. That life changing experience is initiated by God's love and our response of Godly sorrow which is a desire to turn from sin and self and turn toward God.

A while back the phrase "my bad" was used as a quick fix kind of acknowledgment of fault or admission of a mistake. The words, however, seemed shallow and void of any sense of genuine responsibility or sorrow.

Weak, cheap worldly sorrow "don't fix nothing"; it's deadly. Godly sorrow heals relationships with God and man.

Stay in the Game

I have a new friend who is an architect by day and a coach for his son's little league baseball team in the evening. He is excited about coaching and about life. The son is a product and blessing of a second marriage. I sense that Oscar's ability to leave the drawing board at the office for the baseball field is likely a discovery born out of previous family failure, vocational fatigue, and a desire to get it right this time around.

Over the telephone I was telling Oscar one of my favorite children's stories about the little fellow who was standing on second base when his teammate hit the ball into the outfield. He ran from second but stopped at third. From the bleachers he heard his mother shouting, "Go home Johnny, go home." With a perplexed look on his face, he yelled back at his mom, "But the game ain't over yet."

Oscar laughed and said, "That really happened to us." His son had stopped on third base and the assistant coach screamed for him to go home. The little leaguer walked off the base, strolled through the dugout, and was on his way to the car when his dad caught him.

The Apostle Paul having experienced one adversity and rejection after another kept reminding himself that it wasn't over yet. He wrote of being "pressured on every side but not crushed; perplexed, but not in despair; persecuted, but not abandoned; struck down, but not destroyed." He continually encouraged himself and others with the words, "Do not lose heart" (2 Corinthians 4:8-9,16).

Remember, the game "ain't over 'til it's over." The little leaguer knew what he was talking about, and if we are going to play in the big league of life we must learn to stay on the field. Let's make sure that we keep on running.

The Boss Angel

Nell Howell is a retired school teacher who was a member of one of my former churches. Nell loved children and helped us to rear our three. She was gracious in volunteering to stay with our sons when trips would take Jean and me out of town overnight. Nell would quote to our boys from the book of Hezekiah. In case you are looking it up, there is no such book in the Bible. Hezekiah was a less than sanctified collection of anything Nell wanted to say.

Nell's own children lived great distances away. While she enjoyed the trips to see the grandchildren, much of her grandparenting was carried out long distance in cooperation with Ma Bell.

It was about two years ago that Nell told me of a telephone conversation she had with her granddaughter. Lauren was thrilled to get to tell grandmother that she was going to be in the Christmas play at her church. "That's fantastic," the proud grandparent responded. "What part are you going to play?" Lauren thought a moment and then answered, "I'm going to be the boss angel."

During the Advent Season the nativity is reenacted all over the world as Christians prepare to celebrate the birth of

Jesus Christ. Little freckled face boys don their dads' bath robes to become ancient shepherds and wise men. Mothers drape their delicate daughters in bed sheets to look like angels. With enough cotton balls, grocery bags, and Elmer's glue the rest of the kids can be transformed into the full cast including sheep, cows and donkeys.

Appropriately dressed and properly rehearsed, they all find their place around Mary and Joseph and the manger. Even the youngest of the Sunday night stars know that it's the baby in the manger who is the most significant player. After all it was on Him that the Bethlehem star stopped to stare.

The prophet Isaiah, long before the Savior's birth, provided the script for the divine drama: "For unto us a child is born, to us a son is given." We delight when our children take part in the Christmas play depicting the miracle birth of God's Son. Through that birth God reached from heaven to touch all of life with sacred significance. God so loved that He gave a Son. That is the drama of God's redeeming grace, and we are all invited to have a part in His divine pageant. It is in relationship to Him that our search for significance finds cause for celebration.

The Last Word

A young mother had tucked her three year old daughter in bed. All of the nightly bedtime rituals had been accomplished, and yet little Sarah Ashley kept making one request after another. It certainly was not starvation for love and attention but an obvious effort to stall sleep that kept Sarah Ashley asking for another drink of water, another trip to the potty and another good night kiss.

Finally in exasperation the mother sternly said, "Now lay down and go to sleep. I don't want to hear another word out of you and I mean it. Good Night!"

The mother walked from the room flipping the light switch as she left. Exhausted she lay down beside her husband in the bedroom down the hall. Breathing deeply to untie the tensions of a busy day, she hoped to inhale the quietness of the night.

"Mama," the silence was broken. "Can I speak to my daddy, please?" Sarah Ashley wanted another opinion. At three years of age she was testing the limits.

There is a Biblical story of Balak, king of Moab, who sent his servants to summon a prophet by the name of Balaam. Balak wanted Balaam to place a curse on the people of Israel. But Balaam knew the people of Israel to be blessed by God and refused to curse them, saying, "Even if Balak gave me his palace filled with silver and gold, I could not do anything great or small to go beyond the command of the Lord my God" (Numbers 22:18). Balak appealed for another opinion and Balaam consulted God a second and even a third time, but God's word stood firm and His spokesman stood tall. The prophet revealed his own weakness in even going to Moab and in carrying Balak's appeal to God, but in the end Balaam knew that God's word must be his word.

When we don't hear what we want to hear from God, we often turn elsewhere. When our desires find no affirmation in the word of God or the church, we walk away to find support for our self-centered pursuits somewhere else.

Like little Sarah Ashley we want somebody to give us what we want or tell us what we want to hear. Childish rebellion keeps the fearful curtain of darkness falling about us and robs us of peaceful rest in the will of God.

The writer of Psalm 119 acknowledged that all of God's words are true, and then he said so beautifully, "The unfolding of your word gives light." Let God's word be the last word.

The Lord Has Come!

One of our choir teachers had asked the four and five year old choir members to sit in a circle. She said that December was the month in which someone very special had a birthday. Hands were raised. As the choir members were called on, the names of Jimmy, Bob and Susan were mentioned. The teacher responded that these members did have birthdays but there was someone whom we study in the Bible that has a birthday. One hand shot up and when the teacher called on Daniel, he said, "Jesus has a birthday." Michael whispered to Kendall, "We need to send Jesus a birthday card." Kendall immediately responded, "We need to hurry because the postman has to go all the way to heaven!"

Christmas, which is the celebration of Jesus' birthday, is about Jesus coming all the way from heaven to earth. The writers of scripture told a beautiful and simple narrative of the Son of God taking human flesh and form through a miracle birth to a devout Jewish couple, Mary and Joseph. The writer of the gospel of John presented the birth of Jesus with eloquent theological splendor: "In the beginning was the Word, and the Word was with God, and the Word was God.

He was with God in the beginning. The Word became flesh and made His dwelling with us. We have see His glory, the glory of the One and Only, who came from the Father, full of grace and truth."

One of my favorite Christmas carols is "Joy to the World." The full title of the song is "Joy to the World! The Lord Is Come." The words of the hymn that heralds the coming of Jesus call out to the world to receive her king and for every heart to prepare Him room.

Christmas is a reminder that God is not really a long way off but rather has come among us. His name is Emmanuel which means "God with us."

May you feel a fresh closeness of God's spirit as you celebrate Christmas this year. Worship the Lord and experience anew the wonders of His love.

The Mission Project

After we had moved to a new church in Georgia, our young son, Jim, returned to visit with his friends back in South Carolina on several occasions.

During the summer following his first grade of school while staying with his close friend Michael, the boys gathered up their old neighborhood gang and went out canvassing the community for a "worthy cause." They were collecting money for the Lottie Moon Offering for Foreign Missions. At least that's what they said.

One lady became suspicious that these angelic beings might not be on the up and up and asked if they were sure the money was really for foreign missions.

Michael told the lady, "You see this boy. He's Reverend Holley's son, and you know he wouldn't tell a lie." She didn't buy the boys' story, and they were caught at the local service station buying gas to go in a go-cart one of the boys had gotten for Christmas.

Now there was no doubt that these guys were on a mission. The problem was that their mission was to gas up the go-cart so they could enjoy some high speed entertainment. They were certainly not the first nor the last to get tangled up between selfish motivation and worthy missions.

Christianity calls us to rise above selfishness and to share in the needs of others. The coming of Christ was a sacrificial act of God. He saw our need. God's very creation was lost like sheep without a shepherd. He knew we needed help and so he came. He would crawl if he had to, so he came as a baby. He crawled, he cried, he called, he challenged, and then one day he climbed up on a cross and stretched out his arms as if to say, "I love you this much."

May you experience the God who became a babe to be with us and became like us that we could become more like Him. What a Savior!

What We Tell
Our Children

A grandmother told me of her grandson's less than enthusiastic response to our church's Vacation Bible School. "Sean," she had said to him, "the church is having Bible School next week and you will get to go every morning." His reply was, "Grandma, I have gone to Bible School for three years and I have learned everything I need to know."

It sounds like this kid had read Robert Fulghum's book, *All I Really Need to Know I Learned in Kindergarten.* Indeed much of what is vital to life is observed and absorbed at a very early age. Children have such a teachable spirit. They ask questions; they are eager to learn.

Five year olds believe everything their parents tell them and fifteen year olds question anything their parents say. I remember our son coming home from school one day while in the first grade and telling us that the people in Africa live in ice houses called igloos. We had a difficult time convincing him that there was something wrong with his information. He was sure that his teacher had said Africa and that settled it as far as he was concerned.

111

Because our little ones have such an adventuresome spirit and are so eager and willing to learn, we have a window of opportunity to communicate our faith and instill our values. Our homes are the laboratory of life, and every classroom whether at the church or in the school is a launching pad to the future.

Jesus spoke strongly against the abuse of leadership and neglect of responsible guidance in regard to our children. Of those who would mislead a little one, Jesus said, "It would be better for him to be thrown into the sea with a millstone tied around his neck" (Luke 17:2).

Some of us behave as though we decided to drop out after only three years of Bible School, and some of us act like we have gone on vacation from what Biblical truth we may have learned even as children. Our unrestrained liberties have tied us to a millstone of moral relativism and we are drowning in a sea of uncertainty. In such bondage we don't know what to tell the children and we don't bother to tell them anything.

Jesus said, "If you hold to my teachings, you are really my disciples. Then you will know the truth, and the truth will set you free" (John 8:31-32). Tell your children about Jesus. Teach them the truth. Take them to church.

Where Is God?

My wife was trying to explain to one of our sons that God is a spirit being and because God is spirit we cannot see Him. Yet she was quick to explain that although invisible to our sight we can observe the evidence of God's presence about us.

"We see the trees grow and watch the flowers bloom," she reasoned with him.

Out of the clouds of childish innocence he responded, "Oh, I see; God's hiding in the bushes with the birds and bees."

Where in the world is God today? In his book *The Heart of the Problem*, Dr. Henry Brandt talks about "The Myth of Complexity." One of the world's great Christian psychologists, Dr. Brandt calls his readers back to a life transforming faith in God. Out of his own crisis and his counsel with troubled clients over many years Dr. Brandt presents a God who is available and able to touch our hearts with healing love.

Our world is trying everything else. We spend billions of dollars searching for solutions to our problems. Physicians, psychiatrists, psychologists, professors, politicians and preachers put much effort into putting troubled lives back together.

Among many of those helpers who have the best interest of humanity at heart there is a sad conclusion that we work alone in our efforts. As Henry Brandt assesses our culture, he concludes that there is a feeling that we are left to ourselves, "No deity can save us. We must save ourselves." Some folks believe that "God isn't." Others believe "God is" and experience a personal relationship with Him. Open your heart to God. He's not hiding from you.

God's Word tells us, "But if from there you seek the Lord your God, you will find Him if you look for Him with all your heart. (Deuteronomy 4:29)." I believe that and encourage you to turn to the Lord. Trust Him with all of your heart.

Who's Your Coach?

A caring young lady in Metro Atlanta lost her husband recently at an early age. Nancy and her husband had invested much of their time in benevolent work in the community. One of their areas of involvement was a compassionate relationship with a single mother and her son Eli.

With the death of her husband, Nancy spent even more time with Eli, who is considered her godchild. Eli usually spends the evenings with Nancy. She drives him to soccer practice and recently was attempting to prepare Eli for his first soccer game. Nancy made a "fuss" over his new soccer uniform and tried to build his excitement on the upcoming game. She offered her lesson on following the coach's instructions. "Eli, you must pay close attention to what your coach says," she told him. "Whatever the coach tells you to do, you must do it."

Throughout the game Nancy noticed that Eli seemed totally oblivious to the coach's instructions. His instructions got no response from the little guy. Eli played along the sidelines, wandered away from the area where the coach stood and appeared completely disinterested in anything the coach said. Exasperated that her pre-game talk seemed to have accomplished nothing, Nancy was relieved when the game ended.

Later that afternoon as Nancy and Eli drove into their neighborhood, Nancy recognized the soccer coach standing with several other persons at a yard sale. "Look, Eli, it's your coach," she said excitedly. "Where, where's my coach?" Eli asked. "Right there, there in the yard; that's your soccer coach" she said. "Oh" exclaimed Eli, "that's my coach!"

Eli had not deliberately disobeyed Nancy on the soccer field. He had not consciously ignored the coach. He just didn't know the coach and probably did not understand what a coach was.

Jesus said, "I am the good shepherd, I know my sheep and my sheep know me" (John 10:14). The apostle Paul wrote about the "surpassing greatness of knowing Christ." The Christian life is about following Jesus. Christians are to build their lives on the teaching of Jesus. Yet it is impossible to faithfully follow someone that we do not know and trust.

Perhaps the reason that some of us who consider ourselves Christian fall so short of Christ-like behavior is that we don't really know the Christ. It is possible to be religious, to know about Christ, to be involved in church and really not know the Lord in a personal way. Let me encourage you to get to know the Coach.

To order additional copies write or call:

Lamar Holley
Kidstuff
P.O. Box 228
Lawrenceville, GA 30046-0228
770-963-5121
lhlfbc@bellsouth.net